ANIMAL SCAVENGERS

# Wolverines

## SANDRA MARKLE

Lerner Publications Company / Minneapolis

# THE ANIMAL WORLD IS FULL OF SCAVENGERS.

Scavengers are the cleanup crew who find and eat carrion (dead animals) in order to survive. Every day, animals are born and animals die. Without scavengers, the bodies of dead animals would rot away slowly. The decaying flesh would smell bad and take up space. It could also pollute water and attract flies and other disease-carrying insects. Fortunately, scavengers everywhere eat dead and dying animals before they have time to rot. In the forests and open tundra of northern Europe, Siberia, and North America, winters are long and fierce. *In these harsh places, wolverines are part of the scavenger cleanup crew.*

*It's a March evening in northern Canada.* Overhead the full moon paints the craggy peaks of the snow-covered Rocky Mountains with shadows. In the forest lower down the mountains, snowflakes tiny as glitter dust swirl in the frigid wind. A sudden gust loosens snow from the branches of a big pine. Caught in this frosty shower, a female wolverine stops long enough to shake most of the snow off her shaggy coat. As she lopes along, her long body humps up and stretches out like a giant inchworm. It's a pace she can keep up for hours. She easily covers 18 miles (30 kilometers) each night searching for food.

*The female wolverine regularly spreads her urine on the snow* to leave her scent. She also has scent glands along her belly. Dragging her belly along the snow, she deposits another scent signature. Each wolverine has a home range, an area it knows well. These scent markers let other wolverines passing this way know that this area is her home range.

A little farther on, the female detects the strong scent of carrion. She cautiously climbs onto a fallen tree to look around. Then she runs her tongue in and out of her mouth to get a "taste" of scents in the air. A wolverine's view of the world is shaped as much by scents as by sights. As she gets nearer, she detects another scent that keeps her from rushing to the carrion. It is the smell of wolves, predators who kill other animals for food.

*The female wolverine follows her nose slowly and carefully* toward the food and the predator wolves. Even before she sees them, she hears them growling and snarling. She would wait for the wolves to leave, if they seemed to be nearly finished. But they are still competing with each other over their meal.

If the wolves see her, they'll likely attack her. These predators are more than twice her size, so she moves away. Her sharp memory will help her find this spot in the forest again later. When the wolves have eaten their fill and left, she can check out whatever is left of the carcass.

Instead of waiting, she goes to a spot where she has buried leftovers from another meal. With her sturdy claws, she digs through the ice-crusted snow and frozen ground. The fur covering the bottoms of her feet protects her from the sharp bits of ice and cold snow. Finally, she claims her prize— a frozen chunk of deer meat.

The wolverine licks and gnaws the meat until, bit by bit, she thaws it enough to bite some off the bone. She gulps this down and licks and gnaws some more. Wolverines have big, cone-shaped teeth and powerful jaws with strong muscles. After the meat is gone, she crushes the bone to get the marrow inside. She also swallows the bone fragments, which will pass with her wastes.

*By the time the female wolverine has finished eating,* it's snowing again and the wind is howling. She digs a tunnel into a snowbank. Then she crawls inside to sleep while the storm rages outside.

The next day, when the storm is over and the sun is shining, the female emerges. She climbs up into a tree and stretches out on a branch. There she is safe from predators. Shielded from the cold wind by her thick fur coat, she dozes, soaking up the sun's warmth. She sleeps through most of the day, stirring only when a noise wakes her. Then, after looking around, she dozes off again.

*In the evening, the female wolverine wakes up* and climbs down from the tree. Overhead the moon is a glowing silver ball shining on the snow and brightening the sky. The female wolverine can see well in this low light. She has no trouble finding her way back to the remains of the wolf pack's kill. When she gets close, she stops, sniffing the air and listening for danger. The terrain is safe, so she goes to the deer carcass and begins to gnaw on the frozen meat. Soon she detects another scent. A young black bear has awakened from his winter's sleep and is looking for a meal.

*The female wolverine makes an explosive huffing sound.* Startled, the young bear snorts, but he doesn't stop moving toward her and the carcass. The female wolverine growls and releases bad-smelling chemicals from the anal glands under her tail. The bear sniffs the strong, unpleasant odor. He hesitates. Snorting again, the bear lowers his head and attacks. The female wolverine snarls and bites, but she's no match for the bear. She breaks free and sprints away.

*When she feels safe, the wolverine slows to her loping gait.* She continues at this pace as day fades into night. Finally, her sharp sense of smell again guides her to a meal. This time it's a deer that, only hours earlier, died from old age and starvation. The wolverine is the first to find this carrion and quickly digs in.

Hearing a rustling noise, she stops eating and looks up. As she peers into the night, the mirrorlike layer at the back of her eyes makes her eyes gleam in the moonlight. The sound is nothing to worry about, so she goes back to her meal. Tonight, when she's full, there is still some food left over. The female digs a hole in the snow and buries a chunk for another time.

Her next stop is a den she dug to use whenever she is in this part of her home range. The female wolverine quickly digs away the snow that is blocking the den's only entrance. Inside the den is a network of tunnels and chambers. Some of these chambers contain stored food. The wolverine crawls down into one of her sleeping chambers. A few hours later, she gives birth to two babies, called kits.

The little male and female are as tiny as newborn kittens. Their eyes are closed, but they can already detect scents. Crawling toward the scent of their mother's milk, they each locate a nipple on her belly and nurse. Then they burrow into her warm fur and sleep. The wolverine doesn't leave her kits for the first two days of their lives. After that, when hunger forces her to get a meal, she goes to a side tunnel where she has cached (stored) food. With only their thin fur coats to keep them warm, the kits huddle together until their mother returns.

*For the first week of the kits' lives, the female wolverine stays in the den.* She gets food from her cache in the den's chambers. She uses an empty chamber to drop her wastes. By staying close, she keeps the kits warm and lets them nurse frequently. The kits quickly grow to be about hamster size. Woolly gray fur replaces their thin, white birth coats. By the time the female is forced to leave the kits to search for food again, the young wolverines are better able to stay warm on their own. The wolverine doesn't leave for long, though. She only goes far enough to dig up a chunk of a snowshoe hare she'd cached outside before the kits were born.

*By the time the kits are eight weeks old, their eyes are open.* The snow is melting, and the days are much longer. The female carries the kits in her mouth—one by one—to a new den among big boulders. This is the perfect home for the active young wolverines. The ledges are good places to climb and explore. This is play for the kits, but it's also a way for them to build strong muscles and develop coordination. If a wolf, mountain lion, or other predator comes close, the youngsters can scurry inside the den to safety.

By the time the kits are ten weeks old, the female wolverine moves them again. This time their new den is at the base of a tall, dead tree. Inside, there's shelter from the spring rains and a place to hide from predators. When they aren't napping, the kits spend most of their time outside the den. They call to each other with chuckling sounds as they climb and explore the tree's branches.

One day the little male climbs higher than he's ever gone before. When he stops and looks around, he suddenly freezes. He clings to the branch he's on and cries his shrill panic cry, "Mah-mah-mah! Mah-mah-mah!"

*The female wolverine is close enough to hear her kit's distress cry* and comes running. Suddenly, the female spots a big male wolverine. He is heading for her kit. Male wolverines sometimes kill kits they find alone. The female rushes to cut him off. When the two wolverines meet on a fallen tree, the female snarls and stands her ground. The male snarls too. When the female advances, the male leaves. He doesn't want to risk being injured in a fight. The intruder is gone, so the female goes to the tree and calls to her kit. At first, the panicked young male continues to wail. He clings tightly to the tree. The female calls to him again and again. Finally, the little male climbs down. He nuzzles into her fur and nurses.

*The kits stop nursing when they are about three months old.* Born with a set of tiny teeth called milk teeth, the kits are now cutting their adult teeth. Their mother has been giving them a taste of adult food. She hauls home chunks of meat and bone for the kits to gnaw on.

At four months, the youngsters tag along after their mother when she goes foraging. The kits develop their foraging skills by watching their mother. Another lesson they learn is that climbing a tree is a good way to get up high to look around and to escape predators. And when the female carries a deer's leg up a tree, the kits learn a way to protect their food.

By late July, the kits are nearly full-grown and sometimes go foraging alone. The young female finds a place where she saw her mother cache food. She sniffs out the stored food and carries it to a rock to eat it. She stays away for two days before she rejoins her mother.

The young male also goes foraging alone. And when he smells a hare, he sneaks up on it and pounces. This tasty meal teaches the young male that he can overpower and kill prey. He doesn't have to rely only on finding food that's already dead.

In the weeks that follow, the young wolverines continue to forage alone some of the time. Other times, they follow their mother, eating from whatever carcass she is able to find. Then one night, the world changes as the first snow falls, covering the trees and the ground. The young wolverines are suddenly playful again, rolling and tumbling in the snow.

During their first winter, the young wolverines remain in their mother's home range. They benefit from searching an area they already know well. Sometimes, when food is scarce, they trail after their mother and share her cached food supply.

*Toward the end of winter, the young male leaves his mother* and sister. While he's foraging, he wanders into new territory. When he doesn't encounter the scent of other male wolverines, he claims this area for his home range.

The young female forages alone too, but she remains in her mother's home range. She'll share this range for another year or two. Then she'll move farther away and raise a family of her own. Meanwhile, the female wolverine has mated again and three new babies are developing inside her. The wolverine cleanup crew of the tundra and far northern forests has added another generation and is growing strong.

# Looking Back

- Take another look at the wolverine kits on pages 20 and 21. A baby wolverine's coat is a different color than the adult coat. Are they still white by the time they're eight weeks old? Look at the babies on page 25 to find out.

- Look at the wolverines' claws on the title page. Now look through the book to find other photos of wolverines in action. How does having big, sturdy claws help this scavenger?

- Look back through the book to compare what the wolverine's home range looks like during the winter and during the summer. Most wolverine kits are born in the late winter in February or March. Why do you think this helps wolverine kits survive?

# Glossary

ANAL GLANDS: body parts in an animal's hind end that produce chemicals that the animal deposits or sprays out to communicate

CACHE: a place where food is stored

CARRION: a dead animal that a scavenger eats

DEN: a protected place for giving birth, sleeping, and eating. The female wolverine digs a burrow and tunnels and raises her kits there.

HOME RANGE: an area that a wolverine claims and within which it searches for food

KITS: baby wolverines

PREDATOR: an animal that hunts and eats other animals in order to survive

PREY: an animal that a predator catches to eat

SCAVENGER: an animal that feeds on dead animals

SCENT: an odor left behind by an animal

SENSE OF SMELL: an animal's ability to detect odors

TUNDRA: the nearly flat, treeless plain between the Arctic Circle and the forests of North America, Europe, and Siberia

# Further Information

## Books

Brimner, Larry Dane. *Polar Mammals.* New York: Scholastic Library, 1997. Wolverines are included in this look at how animals are adapted to face the challenge of life in polar regions.

Day, Trevor. *Taiga.* Oxford, UK: Raintree/Steck Vaughn Publishers, 2003. Text and illustrations provide an in-depth look at the northern forests where some of the tallest trees in the world grow and where wolverines live.

Somerville, Barbara. *Animal Survivors of the Arctic.* New York: Scholastic Library, 2004. This book provides a closer look at the Arctic ecosystem, the wolverines and other animals living there, and how animals with reduced populations are making a recovery.

## Videos

*Arctic Kingdom—Life at the Edge.* Washington, DC: National Geographic, 1998. This film dramatically depicts one of the most challenging environments on earth and looks at how wolverines and other animals survive there.

*Wild Europe: Wild Arctic.* Boston: WGBH, 2000. This film examines wolverines and other animals that make the Arctic their home and provides a close look at this ecosystem.

## Website

*The Alaska Zoo.*
http://www.alaskazoo.org/willowcrest/wolverineshome.htm
This website gives information about wolverines in the wild and has photos and text about Wilbur and Jenny, wolverines in this zoo.

# Index

*With love for good friends Keith and Marion McQuillan*

The author would like to thank Craig Gardner, Howard Golden, and Jack Whitman, wildlife biologists with the Alaska Department of Fish and Game Division of Wildlife Conservation; and Dr. Audrey Magoun, principal investigator for the Wolverine Project's study of wolverine kits, project leader for the Living Legacy Trust Boreal Wolverine Project, and co-director of the Wolverine Foundation, also of the Alaska Department of Fish and Game. The author would also like to express a special thank-you to Skip Jeffery for his help and support during the creative process.

## Photo Acknowledgments

The photographs in this book are used with permission of: © Antti Leinonen, pp. 1, 3, 5, 7, 10, 11, 19, 23, 31, 33, 37; © Michael H. Francis, pp. 9, 25, 26, 27; © Dale Pedersen, pp. 13, 20, 21, 29, 32, 35; © Daniel J. Cox/naturalexposures.com, pp. 15, 17, 34.
Front Cover: © Daniel J. Cox/naturalexposures.com.
Back cover (top): © Dale Pedersen. Back cover (bottom): *Army Ants*: © Christian Ziegler; *Hyenas*: © Richard du Toit/naturepl.com; *Jackals*: © Beverly Joubert/National Geographic/Getty Images; *Tasmanian Devils*: Photodisc Royalty Free by Getty Images; *Vultures*: © Chris Hellier/CORBIS; *Wolverines*: © Daniel J. Cox/naturalexposures.com.

Lerner Publications Company
A division of Lerner Publishing Group
241 First Avenue North
Minneapolis, MN 55401

Website address: www.lernerbooks.com

Library of Congress Cataloging-in-Publication Data

Markle, Sandra.
    Wolverines / by Sandra Markle.
      p.   cm. — (Animal scavengers)
    Includes bibliographical references and index.
    ISBN-13: 978−0−8225−3198−2 (lib. bdg. : alk. paper)
    ISBN-10: 0−8225−3198−4 (lib. bdg. : alk. paper)
    1. Wolverine—Juvenile literature.  I. Title.  II. Series: Markle, Sandra. Animal scavengers.
  QL737.C25M29  2005
  599.76'6—dc22                                                    2004029670

Manufactured in the United States of America
1 2 3 4 5 6 − DP − 10 09 08 07 06 05

READ ANIMAL PREDATORS, A *BOOKLIST* TOP 10 YOUTH NONFICTION SERIES BY SANDRA MARKLE

Crocodiles
Great White Sharks
Killer Whales
Lions
Owls
Polar Bears
Wolves